THE TURNING POINT

ONE DOES NOT BECOME SUCCESSFUL BY CHANCE. CHANGE YOUR MINDSET, CHANGE YOUR LIFE.

DEGOL S. TEKESTE

TABLE OF CONTENTS

About The Author	v
Acknowledgments	ix
Prologue	1
1. Invest In Yourself	3
2. The 80/20 Rule	9
3. Believe In Yourself And In Your Goals	13
4. Self Confidence Is Key	18
5. The Importance Of A Daily Routine	24
6. You Make & Break Your Day Between 5–7 AM	29
7. Highlight Your Progress	34
8. Social Media And Your Mental Health	41
9. Reprogram Your Subconscious Mind	48
10. The Art Of Communicating	52
11. The Art Of Communicating: Part 2	63
12. Mind Over Matter	79
13. The 21/90 Rule	81
14. Fear: False Evidence Appearing Real	86
15. Overcome Fear And Build Confidence	90
16. Failure Is Bound To Happen	96
17. Self Discipline	101
18. Live With A Sense Of Urgency	106

ABOUT THE AUTHOR

Degol S. Tekeste is a knowledge seeker who studies personal development. In his quest for financial independence, he inspires and encourages all to seek greatness within themselves. He resides in California.

-Inspiring Greatness

Copyright © 2022 by Degol S. Tekeste

All rights reserved. No part of this book may be reproduced, distributed, or transmitted in any form or by any means, including photocopying, recording, or other electronic or mechanical methods, without the prior written permission of the author, except in the case of brief quotations embodied in critical reviews and certain other noncommercial uses permitted by copyright law.

DEDICATION

To all whom I love.

ACKNOWLEDGMENTS

This book came into existence when I had the opportunity to follow and study my mentor and his habits. What I learned from him forever altered the trajectory of my life. As I started to apply these habits and lessons to my day to day life, I began to see differences in all areas of my life.

PROLOGUE

Most people laugh when they hear that success is a choice. Then again, most people are nowhere near as successful as they think they are. The Turning Point illustrates the necessary steps and actions anyone can apply in hopes of attaining success. Imparted with practical life lessons and scientific studies, The Turning Point is an inspirational book that brings new relevance to the old proverb-life presents us many choices, the choices we make today determines our future.

1

INVEST IN YOURSELF

Times have changed. In today's world, one who lacks riches seldom survives. According to Elizabeth Warren (Senator of Mass.), 0.1% of the US population owns about as much as the bottom 90% of the US population. To put this figure in perspective, that's nearly 200,000 families that own more wealth than the remaining 90% of the US population (about 110 million US families).

That's preposterous, especially in this day and age. Unfortunately, a wealth disparity between social classes has existed since the beginning of time and will continue to exist until the very end. Understanding why a wealth disparity occurs in the first place is key to understanding why the gap between the haves, and the have nots exists. In this world of "now," each one of us have the resources and freedom to achieve and accomplish all that our hearts desire but fail to do so. Why? Because as residents of the greatest nation in the world, we fail to take advantage of the opportunities that are presented to us. We're too picky.

We simply want the best of the best without putting any work in. As a result, the majority of people lack the skills and tools needed to accumulate their own wealth. To simply put it, we're too lazy. Even so, it's never too late to start. If you truly want to have more in life, you have to become more. Remember, empty pockets never held anyone back, only empty heads and empty hearts can do that.

Invest In Yourself

It's often said that formal education will make you a living wage, but self-education will yield you a fortune. The number one and quickest way one can attain success is by simply investing in oneself. The top 10 people on the Forbes list all have one thing in common. They all became successful by simply investing in themselves. Jeff Bezos, Bill Gates, Warren Buffett, Mark Zuckerberg and so on all invested in themselves.

Contrary to popular belief, success can be attained by anyone who seeks it. As long as you are willing to work harder on yourself than you do on your job, you too can attain success. You need not be successful to start, but you have to start to be successful. There are countless ways one can invest in themselves. From self-knowledge to personal development, investing in oneself is a sure way to achieve success.

For example, one can enroll in classes at the local community college to earn credits toward a lucrative college degree or a job certification. You can also invest in private lessons to help master a new skill or even brush up an area in your life which you are weak at. You have to make it your personal goal to be the best in your field in order to be successful.

Whatever you decide to do in life, make it your top priority to be the best. Don't view your current job as trading time for money unless your ultimate goal is to work for the rest of your life. Instead, in your spare time, look for ways to increase your income.

For instance, you can invest in a small business while still working at your job. You can do this by simply using a part of the income you earn to funnel your new business. Who knows, it could wind up surpassing your current salary by earning more than you ever imagined. The main goal here is to simply generate multiple streams of income. If one fails, you can always rely on the other.

Pay Off Debt

The one thing that can undoubtedly hinder your chances of becoming successful is debt. According to Experian, the total credit card debt has increased by 6% in 2019, reaching 807 Billion in the US. In addition, 60.5 percent of the US population have credit cards with the average person carrying around 6,028 dollars in credit card debt.

In order to eliminate debt, it's best to focus on paying off high-interest debt first. These are the debts that seem to increase day in and day out, even after making your routinely monthly payments. Credit cards, car loans, payday loans and student loans all fall into this one category.

They're's simply no investments greater than paying off your high-interest debt. They are designed to keep you at bay at all costs. High-interest debts are revolving doors linked directly to your savings accounts, where your money enters and disappears. In order to eliminate debt, make it your number one priority to pay off high-interest debt.

Set Smart Goals

When writing down your daily, weekly, monthly or yearly goals, make sure they fit the S.M.A.R.T goals standards. Doing this will save you time down the road by eliminating unrealistic goals.

- S — Specific (Significant).
- M — Measurable (Meaningful).
- A — Attainable (Action-Oriented).
- R — Relevant (Rewarding).
- T — Time-bound (Trackable).

How To Apply S.M.A.R.T Goals

For example, instead of writing down "I want to save 50,000 dollars" as a goal. Change it too, "I plan on saving 50,000 dollars by January 1, 2025." This way, you have a more definite and attainable goal. If you haven't already started setting goals, start now. As you implement this into your daily routine, you'll find your income gradually increasing. Over time, by practicing setting S.M.A.R.T goals, you will eventually see improvements in all aspects of your life.

Live Below Your Means

Spend less money than you earn. It's as simple as that. This is a crucial step to creating wealth. As long as you are spending less than you are bringing in, you'll always be on top of your finances. This is an important step people overlook.

Nearly 60% of the population fails to do this. According to a survey conducted by Charles Schwab, a whopping 59% of Americans reported living paycheck to paycheck. This fact implies that people are spending their money as fast as they are making it.

Furthermore, only 28% of Americans reported having a written financial plan. Budgeting is key to making all this work. A person without a plan is planning to fail. You must account for every penny that you make. A well thought out budget will help you track your finances. Having a written budget also helps you to cut back on miscellaneous expenses.

As a result, your spending decreases while your income increases. In other words, the less money you spend, the more you have to invest.

Lastly, avoid lifestyle inflation. As your income increases (which is bound to happen), you have to remain committed to your budget. Do not increase your spending. You have to be disciplined and true to your budget no matter how much your income increases. As the saying goes, "more money more problems."

Take Risks

If you are not willing to risk the unusual, you will have to settle for an ordinary life. Nothing great was ever achieved without risk. Failure is bound to happen. Accept these terms and keep trying. The law of averages simply states that if you do something long enough, you will eventually succeed. Thomas Edison proved this. Do not give up after your first failed attempt. You will never attain success.

Instead, analyze your mistakes and draw up a new game plan. Failure is the first step to success. You have to know what doesn't work in order to identify what does. It's a process that requires a little bit of faith and persistence.

2

THE 80/20 RULE

The 80/20 rule was first discovered in 1897, by Italian economist Vilfredo Pareto. His discovery has since been referred to as the Pareto Principle, the Pareto Law, the 80/20 Rule, the Principle of the Least Effort and the Principle of Imbalance. This Principle alone has helped shape the modern world today. Yet, for some unknown reason, it has managed to remain one of the greatest kept secrets of our time.

The 80/20 Rule should be applied by everyone in their day to day life. It can drastically help individuals and groups accomplish more, with less effort. For instance, the 80/20 Rule can raise personal effectiveness and happiness if applied correctly. How is this idea possible?

Well, the 80/20 Rule states that a minority of causes leads to a majority of the results. In other words, this means that 80 percent of what you achieve in your work derives from 20 percent of the time spent. Thus, for all practical purposes, four-fifths of the effort is irrelevant. This idea is contrary to what people normally expect.

What Exactly Is The 80/20 Rule

The 80/20 Rule states that there is an inbuilt imbalance between causes and results, inputs and outputs, and effort and reward. A good benchmark for this imbalance is provided by the 80/20 relationship.

A typical pattern will show that 80 percent of outputs result from 20 percent of inputs, that 80 percent of consequences flow from 20 percent of causes, or that 80 percent of results come from 20 percent of effort.

In business, many examples of the 80/20 Principle has been validated. For example, 20 percent of products usually account for about 80 percent of sales ($) value. 20 percent of products or customers usually accounts for about 80 percent of a business profit. This principle can also be applied to crime, car accidents, education qualifications and much more.

For example, in society today, 20 percent of criminals account for approximately 80 percent of the value of all crime. 20 percent of motorists cause about 80 percent of all accidents. 20% of students achieved 80% of the available educational qualifications.

Also, at home, 20 percent of your carpets are likely to get 80 percent of the wear and tear/traffic. 20 percent of your clothes will be worn 80 percent of the time.

Why The 80/20 Rule Works

THE NUMBER one reason the 80/20 rule is so valuable is that it has been proven to work. It's counterintuitive. We tend to expect that all causes will have roughly the same significance. All customers are equally valuable. That all products and every dollar/sales revenue is as good as another. All employees in a particular category have roughly the same value. That each day, weeks or years we spend has the same significance.

That all our friends and family have roughly equal value to us. That one college is as good as another. That all opportunities are of roughly equal value. This idea is not the case. This response is a false narrative and belief that has been conditioned and instilled in us through time. We've subconsciously become domesticated to these beliefs.

We tend to assume that 50 percent of causes or inputs will account for 50 percent of results or outputs. Although this idea seems like a logical, correct answer, it's far from the truth even though sometimes it may be valid. This 50/50 fallacy is one of the most inaccurate and harmful assumptions one can make.

The 80/20 Rule asserts that when two sets of data, relating to causes and results, can be examined and analyzed, the most likely result is that there will be a pattern of imbalance. The imbalance can derive from any set of numbers. The numbers may be 65/35, 70/30, 75/25, 80/20, 95/5, or 99.9/0.1, or any set of numbers in between.

However, the two numbers in the comparison need not have to tally up to 100. The 80/20 Rule also asserts that when we know the true relationship, we are likely to be surprised at how unbalanced it is. Whatever the actual level of imbalance, it is likely to exceed our prior estimate.

For instance, business owners may already be aware of the fact that some customers and some products are more profitable than others, but when confronted with the extent of the difference, they are left dumbfounded by the results. Furthermore, we may feel that some of our time is valuable than the rest, but if we measure inputs and outputs, the data will further validate this claim.

Whether you realize it or not, the 80/20 Rule applies to your life, to your business, to your social life and to your work. Understanding the 80/20 Rule can give you great insight into understanding the world around you. The 80/20 rule can completely change your life. One can be more efficient, decisive, productive and happier by simply implementing and applying the 80/20 Rule in their life.

3

BELIEVE IN YOURSELF AND IN YOUR GOALS

You've read all the self help books you can get your hands on and watched all the motivational videos in the hopes of bettering yourself. You've spent countless of hours, day in and day out listening to those motivational videos saying, "Never give up, and you'll get what you want!" You've done it all, and nothing is working for you. At the end of the day, you still left wondering, "What is it that I don't have?"

Here's the reality, success is something within you. It's your daily habits. Your morning routines. What you spend the most of your time doing. It's not these tips and tricks that others try to sell you, it's the small choices you make every day!

Learn To Accept Change

Most people think it takes a long time to change. It may

take a long time to decide to change, but change is immediate and instant. With that in mind, wouldn't it be wise if you were to finally squash the fear of change all together? If you don't like how things are in life, change it.

Successful people in life are able to adapt and adjust to change. They need to be. If one idea fails, which many will, the successful mind can adapt.

How does one accept change? As you always have, you just get on with it. Know that it's there, it's happening all the time, and don't let it catch you off-guard. Plan for it, expect it, embrace it, and use it to your advantage. Everything else will fall in place as intended.

Reach Your Goals Everyday

You know that feeling you get when you draw up a To-do list, and you tick each item of it? Think back to the feeling of each of those ticks. Think about how empowered and motivated you feel for the next task. It's a pretty damn good feeling, right? Staring at that completed list at the end of the day, knowing that you've accomplished everything you wanted to do for that day. Make your goals that size. Reach your goals every day. Allow that momentum to build up every single day. If you go to work on your goals every day, your goals will go to work on you.

Start To Commit

Get rid of those committal fears. If you want to be successful, you have to commit to things. A new job, a new partner, a new exercise regime or even a new friendship. Whatever it is, you need to commit! If you can't commit when things are going well, you're definitely not going to be around when stuff hit the fan. You have to stick around long enough to reap the fruits of your labor.

Identify Your Purpose

A purpose is a fast track to success. With your purpose in mind, much like setting S.M.A.R.T. goals, all that hard work seems a lot more appealing to overcome. When things get rough, you can just sit there and say, "Why am I doing this again?" Your purpose will always serve as the motivation you need to keep going. So how do you find your purpose?

Answer these simple questions, brutal honesty required. Who are you? What do you want from life? What is it you have that others will benefit from receiving? How are you going to get there?

Believe In Yourself and In Your Goals

It's timeless advice. You have probably heard it a million times before, but this time you need to let it sink in. If you want to be successful, you have to believe in yourself. Don't believe in yourself because it's your destiny to be successful. Don't believe in yourself because you've got a foolproof plan. Don't believe in yourself because you really want it. Believe in yourself because you know that you're going to put in the work.

Believe in yourself because you know as long you're still breathing, you will continue to work towards your goals. Believe in yourself because you know you'll overcome the next obstacle you're presented with.

In other words, see it and then become it. With this level of self-belief, anything is achievable. You just have to keep your mind fixated on the end goal.

Cultivate Patience

This is another timeless piece of advice one can apply in life. You need to have patience. Yes, some things can happen overnight, but these are often the smaller successes.

It doesn't matter what it is you want to achieve, knowing how to cultivate patience will be a part of it. A successful blog does not launch with thousands of subscribers overnight. A powerful novel does not get written in a day. A fitness model does not miraculously sculpt his or her physique in 24 hours. Success takes time.

Think of success as a plant. If you water a seed for long, it will grow. If you stay down and grind for long, it will show. It's inevitable. You just have to be willing to be patient and continue taking every step you can towards your goals.

Identify Your Downfalls

No successful mind is successful if it cannot see where it falls short. Knowing you're lazy and doing something about the laziness are two very different things. To be successful, you have to identify that laziness, then apply a proactive solution to it. Saying, "Yeah I'm lazy," is not going to get the work done. Also, you're not going to get it perfect the first try. That's okay, as long as you're actually doing something about your downfalls, other than complaining, you are ahead of most.

Choose A Worthy Goal To Pursue

Success does not mean a hefty bank account or a lavish lifestyle. Success is a progressive realization of a worthy goal/ideal. The door to door salesman is as successful as the Doctor operating in the intensive care unit. They are both progressively moving towards a worthy goal/ideal. Who determines whether the goal is worthy? You do. As long as you are progressively moving toward your goals, you too are successful.

∼

4
SELF CONFIDENCE IS KEY

Have you ever wonder what makes a particular person confident? Or, perhaps you may ask yourself this question, how does a confident person act? Well, for starters, confident people acknowledge and celebrate other people successes as if it was their own. They don't envy or get jealous at the sight of other people's success.

Confident people embrace it and in return use it as motivation to further their own success. Other traits of highly confident people include being assertive, cordial and most importantly, being comfortable being themselves.

Don't Hesitate

Hesitation leads too indecision. Confident people roll the dice, take risks and are known for being assertive. This means that they know what they want, when they want it and how to get it. Taking immediate action and not second guessing one's abilities is a clear indication one possess confidence. They're cordial and optimistic about life.

Highly confident people have a knack of choosing a path and sticking to it no matter the circumstances. They're not constantly jumping from one decision to another without making a clear choice on what they want to do. Confident people make their decisions quickly and change their minds slowly. Failures make their decisions slowly and change their minds quickly.

Be Yourself

I think this one is pretty obvious. People who are confident don't try to act in a fake manner, or try to mimic someone else in order to seem "cool" or better than who they really are, simply because they appreciate themselves enough to realize that they are good enough. Confident people don't need to put up a front or a persona to impress others. Confident people are comfortable being themselves and strive to better themselves day in and day out. They take pride in being authentic and true to their ideas and beliefs.

Defend Your Ideas And Beliefs

Confidence means acknowledging and accepting when you're in the wrong, and changing your ideas/beliefs if they aren't off any value. But it also means knowing when to keep them despite what anyone has to say, because many times, you'll be faced with rejection from people for not sharing the same beliefs and ideas.

That's when you have stand up for your beliefs and not let anyone convince you otherwise. You've to be assertive and confident whenever your ideas/beliefs are being challenged. Conforming and switching up too quickly portraits an image of low self confidence in one's ideas and beliefs.

Have A Sense of Direction In Life

Have a game plan drawn out that you can retrieve and look over at any given moment. Having your goals written out means that you are fully aware of what you want in life, and that you have a plan to get to where you want to go. It's hard to be confident about your life, and yourself in general, if you don't even know where your life is headed. It needs not be set on stone but rather in paper where you can tweak it when applicable. The key here is to have a sense of direction in your life.

For this example, I want you to picture two sail boats getting ready to sail. One sailboat has a captain, a destination point and map. The other sailboat has a captain, a destination point and no map. Whom do you think will reach their destination point first?

It's pretty obvious, the captain who has the map will reach his destination point 99.9 percent of the time. The other captain will be lucky to make it out the docking area. The moral of the story here is, if you don't take the time to carefully plan and design your life, chances are you'll fall into someone else's plan. And guess what they have planned for you, not much.

In order to achieve success, you have to carefully plan and design your life. You can't be aimlessly drifting at sea hoping to reach your destination.

Don't Be Easily Influenced

Not all influence is bad, some people can change your life for the better. The key is knowing who to follow and who not to follow. You cannot allow yourself to follow people just because other people are doing so.

If you're an individual who is easily manipulated and influenced by others, you probably lack self confidence in yourself and in your ideas/beliefs. Being resistance to influence means that you know who you are as an individual. This means that you know what you stand for, and aren't afraid to let it be known.

Letting other people dictate your ideas and beliefs in any way, shape or form, is a clear sign of a lack of confidence. One has to keep in mind that opinions of others are one of the cheapest commodities in life, everyone has one, but only yours matter.

Be Comfortable With Being Yourself

Confident people are comfortable in their own skin. They avoid seeking approval and comparing themselves to others. They truly believe that they are good enough to be loved and accepted by others. They don't pretend to be someone else and encourage others to be themselves. They avoid judging others and accept people as they come.

In order to be comfortable with yourself, you first have to learn to love yourself unconditionally. This response means that you accept yourself as you are. That you believe that you can be whatever you want, and that you are good enough without constantly seeking approval or feeling inferior to others. You can simply put it this way, you love being you.

Don't Seek Approval

Most people turn to others in order to reassure themselves that whatever they're doing is "right". This response is a clear sign of seeking validation. Confident people have faith in their work and in their abilities to complete the task at hand. They don't seek validation from others. If you're genuinely confident, you don't need someone to tell you that you're right, because you already know it. Highly confident people take pride in whatever they do in life. They are not afraid to make mistakes and are always looking for ways to better themselves. Whether that be at work or school, confident people refrain from seeking approval from others.

Accept Yourself Unconditionally

Learn how to be happy with who you are while you pursue all that you desire. Being able to live your life on your own terms without caring about what others think or say about you is a major sign of self confidence. In order to acquire confidence, one has to first master the self. How does one do this? By simply acknowledging and accepting yourself as you are, unconditionally. This is the first step of acquiring and achieving self confidence.

5

THE IMPORTANCE OF A DAILY ROUTINE

Hal Elrod once said, your morning routine (or lack of) dramatically affects your levels of success in every single area of your life. Waking up early in the morning with a purpose is a great feeling. Waking up early without a purpose is not. It creates chaos and wastes valuable time. That's why it's important to establish and follow a daily routine. It saves you time and frees up your schedule. From forming new habits to boosting one's productivity levels, establishing a daily routine can positively impact your life.

Forms New Habits

The hardest thing for the human brain to do is to form a new habit. On the other hand, the hardest thing for the human brain to do is to kick a habit. Either way you look at it, one thing is for certain. Habits are a pain in the butt. They can propel you too heights previously thought unattainable or drag you down to depths previously thought attainable. Pick and choose wisely.

When creating and forming your new daily routine, double check and triple check the things you have jotted down on your list. It takes 90 days for one to make a new habit a lifestyle. Make sure that the new habits you're forming are not habits that are going to drag you down. Following a daily routine guarantees and establishes new habits.

Maximizes Productivity Levels

One thing that is for certain when following a daily routine is the fact that it maximizes productivity levels. Following a daily routine ensures that one is not wasting valuable time on miscellaneous tasks. By following a daily routine, you establish control in your life. You basically know the what, who, where, when and why beforehand. Knowing these ahead of time can save time and reduce anxiety levels. You'll quickly come to the realization that following a daily routine helps one get more work done and clears tasks off the to do list. It's a life saving concept that everyone should incorporate into their life.

Lessens Anxiety

Anxiety hinders and limits too many people from achieving and conquering their goals. It's a feeling that can only be understood and examined by experiencing it firsthand. Words alone can't formulate or describe the emotions' anxiety generates. Anxiety is an invisible glass ceiling that stunts and limits one from climbing and reaching the summit. Knowing what you are going to do for the day lessens and decreases anxiety levels drastically. One doesn't have to worry or anticipate their next move. It's a great feeling that creates sense and gives purpose to one's life. It leaves you feeling in control and accomplished at the end of the day.

Boosts Self-Confidence

Going through life with a definite routine can drastically boost one's self-confidence. It will leave people questioning and wondering what it is that you know that they don't. That's what forming and establishing a daily routine instills in you. This gives one a sense of purpose and belonging. It can be a simple thing such as waking up early, exercising daily or reading 10 pages a day. Whatever it may be, establishing a daily routine can drastically improve one's confidence.

An Ideal Daily Routine:

- Wake up at 5 a.m.
- Meditate/exercise
- Make breakfast
- Pack lunch for work
- Be on time to work

- Check/reply to emails/phone calls
- Warm up/make dinner
- Logout/silent all social media by 8pm
- Review paperwork for the day
- Unwind for the day (reading, meditating, etc.)
- Set out work clothes for tomorrow
- Be in bed by 10pm

Make Small Lists

Your ideal list should be NO LONGER than 10-15 items. It's best to keep your list short in the beginning and add on as you get a hang of it. This is not a step by step outline of your day. It's just a rough guideline to help one go through the day. This is about establishing a daily routine to help you balance your work, life, and family time. Your weekends might vary depending on your planning (chores, shopping trips, etc.).

Pace Yourself

Life is a marathon, not a sprint. Don't try to do everything perfectly. Some Days are going to be more unbearable than others. It's okay to skip out on somethings on your list. So instead of stressing out about it, simply jot down what you would like your ideal daily routine to look like. Again, don't aim for anything over the top right now like "waking up at 4:00 a.m daily" or "join a gym and train seven times a week." You'll be setting yourself up for failure and disappointment. Instead, make your ideal list as simple as you can in order to get the flow of things. If you're starting at zero, let's make this attainable. Start slow and gradually increase your intensity level as you go. It takes patience and dedication to be able to establish and follow a daily routine.

6

YOU MAKE & BREAK YOUR DAY BETWEEN 5–7 AM

The early bird gets the worm. It's a saying that many of us are too familiar with. If you were to conduct a survey with all the successful people in your life, you'll quickly come to the realization that waking up early is one trait that they all have in common. It's a simple trait that can transform and positively impact your life significantly. From getting more work accomplished to getting back in shape. Getting up early can drastically transform one's life.

How To Maximize Your Time

There's no such thing as extra time. We all get the same 24 hours a day. Contrary to popular believe, there are ways one can significantly maximize their output levels. By simply adjusting your bedtime, you'll discover that you have all the time in the world you could ever ask for. For example, waking up an hour earlier each day is equivalent to six and a half 40 hour work weeks a year. To put this in perspective, that's a month and a half of "extra time" to do whatever it is you wish. One can write, read, study, meditate, paint, exercise, cook, learn a new language or master a new skill, by simply waking up an hour earlier each day. Time well spent translates to more money to spend, more money to save, and more time on the golf course.

Why You Should Wake Up Early

What you do between the hours of 5–7 a.m. determines your success in life. Most people Operate on A 9–5 schedule. With that in mind, waking up at 5 a.m. automatically puts you ahead of the pack. What one decides to do with in that time frame, is ultimately what ends up making or breaking ones day.

Productivity

Productivity is key. One can wake up early in the morning only to end up binge watching their favorite TV show on Netflix. There's nothing wrong with that. Anyhow, that same individual can't expect to get ahead of the pack by simply laying around. What one puts in is what one gets back. You reap what you sow. It's the law. Like the law of gravity, it works every time. You don't have to understand it to know exactly how it works. It just does.

In other words, Ignorance is not bliss. Ignorance is poverty. To ensure that you are productive, get in the habit of writing down the tasks you want to accomplish. To accomplish this, set the task block in your daily routine. The task block is more or less of a written schedule. Tasks that are written down in a task block are twice as likely to be completed.

While everyone else is tucked in tight, you have the opportunity and freedom to accomplish all that your heart desires. By taking advantage of the "extra time," one can work on improving themselves. For example, you can read. One of the fastest ways to learn something is by reading.

Reading one book can save you years. It's often said, learning from personal experiences is the key to success. While that is indeed the truth, experience is not the best teacher. The best teacher is learning from other people's experiences. By reading about the lives of great people, you can unlock the secrets to what made them great. Learning from other people's past experiences and failures is the key to financial success. It's a shortcut that many people fail to realize and use. It can save you years and even decades of failure and misery. So get in the habit of reading. All great leaders are readers.

Avoid reading the easy books, you may be entertained by them, but you will never grow from them. Instead, read the kinds of books that will help you awaken the greatness within.

Exercise

Exercising is another activity one can perform in the early hours. It's an effective and healthy way to kick start the day. It's typically at the top of the to-do list for many of us. Unfortunately, we never get the chance to cross it off the list. How many times have you heard your friends and relative say "this year, my new year's resolution is to get back in shape." Probably more than you can count. If we are being honest, the most of them were never in shape to begin with. Let alone get "back in shape." So get in the habit of taking care of your body, you only get one.

By waking up early, one can work on and improve their physical appearance drastically. People will wonder how you were able to accomplish so much with so "little time."

The truth is, we have all the time in the world we could possibly need. We are usually too lazy to make use of it all. By waking up early in the morning, you'll come to the realization that time is not scarce, but abundant.

Tips on Getting Up Early

Let's not kid ourselves. Waking up early can be a daunting task. Like any new habit, it's going to be difficult at first. You'll find your body too weak to operate. However, you must push yourself with the desire to excel at your highest ability. One day, you'll find yourself living a life one could have only imagined. Remember, being disciplined and motivated is key to making it all work.

Here's How To Get Started:

1. Go to bed early
2. Put all electronic away during bed time
3. Set your alarm clock & place it out of reach

4. Avoid hitting the snooze button
5. Force yourself to get up
6. Do not rationalize
7. Make it a reward

There's No Such Thing As Extra Time

We all have 24 hours a day. What you choose to do with them is entirely up to you. There's no changing that. We all know time is one of the most valuable commodity in life. There's nothing more valuable and intangible as time. No matter how much riches one has accumulated, time spent can NEVER be bought back. For that reason alone, one should look for ways to maximize every passing hour to their advantage. Waking up early each day is one way to reassure that. It's a small sacrifice that goes a long way. It can yield riches in abundance.

∽

7

HIGHLIGHT YOUR PROGRESS

Everyone has a behavior they'd like to change. Whether that be giving up smoking or cutting back on late night snacking. We certainly all want to change that behavior in a timely matter. If you're trying to quit smoking, most people in a monologue, will say, "smoking kills."

Or if you're trying to drop the extra weight, you might tell yourself, "If I don't lose weight, I might die of obesity." What we're trying to do here is we're trying to scare ourselves and others into changing their behavior. It's not just us, it's society as a whole.

We all share this deep rooted belief that if you threaten people, it will get them to act. Though that might seem like a reasonable assumption, studies reveal that warning signs have little to no impact on behavioral change. For instance, studies have shown that warning signs and images on cigarette packages do not deter smokers from smoking.

On average, warning signs have a minimum effect on changing one's behavior. Matter fact, one study found that when people looked at warning signs, quitting became a lower priority for smokers.

Why Are We Resistant To Warnings?

If something scares us, we tend to shut down and eliminate that negative feelings immediately. We also seek comfort by rationalizing our actions.

For example, you might tell yourself: "My grandpa smoked since he was ten and he lived to be 100 years old. I've really good genes and so I've nothing to worry about."

Or, you might tell yourself: "What's the point about worrying about something that might happen? We're all going to die eventually."

This process can actually make you feel more resilient than you did before, which is why warnings sometimes have this boomerang effect.

The Experiment

An experiment was conducted with about 100 college students to estimate the likelihood of 80 different negative events that might happen to the participants in the future. Participants were asked "What is the likelihood that you'll suffer vision loss in your future?" The majority of participants answered "I think it's about 50%." Afterwards, those participant were given two different expert opinions. Expert A, opinion: "You know, for someone like you, I think it's only 40%." This statement gave the participants an optimistic view of their future.

Expert B opinion: "You know, for someone like you, I actually think it's about 60%. This statement gave the participants a pessimistic view of their future. What researchers found was that people tend to change their beliefs towards a more favorable opinion. In other words, people tend to listen to positive information.

A couple months later, the same experiment was conducted with participants ranging from the ages of 10-80. The results remained the same. In all these age groups, people take in information they want to hear.

Researchers also discovered that kids and teenagers were the worse at learning from bad news, and the ability only progressed as people aged. Even so, it doesn't matter what age you are. One can be 10, 23, 37, 42, 50 or 60. Everyone takes in information they want to hear more than information that they don't want to hear. In the end, we end up with a distorted view of ourselves and life in general.

OUR MISTAKE AS STUDENTS, teachers, parents, mentors, and as employers, is that instead of working with this positive image that people so effortfully maintain, we try and put a clear mirror in front of ourselves and others. We tell them: "You know, the future is just going to get worse and worse." This place doesn't work because the brain will frantically try to distort that image until it gets the image it's happy with. Instead, what if we went along with how our brain works and not against it?

The Intervention

In another study, a hospital installed a camera to monitor how often the medical staff sanitizes their hands before and after entering a patient's room. The medical staff being studied was aware of the cameras being installed.

Even so, only one in ten washed their hands before and after entering a patient's room. Afterwards, an intervention was introduced. Researchers developed an electronic board that showed the medical staff how well they were doing.

Every time the hospital staff washed their hands, the numbers went up on the screen, illustrating the rate of current and weekly shifts progress. What happened next was astonishing.

Compliance raised to staggering 90%. The researchers were amazed as well. So amazed that they made sure to replicate the experiment in another department in the hospital.

Why does this intervention work so well? It works well because instead of using warnings about bad things that can happen in the future, like the spread of diseases, it focuses on monitoring and rewarding positive actions, which inevitably effects the human mind and behavior.

Social Incentives

Social incentives have been proven to have a positive effect on changing behavior. In the hospital study, the medical staff was observant of what other people were doing.

As social creatures, we really care about what other people are doing. Not only do we feel inclined to do as others do, but we want to do the same thing and we want to do it better.

A study led by Ph.D student Micah Edelson showed that upon hearing opinions from others, a signal in the emotional center of our brain gets activated. That signal can predict how likely you are to conform over time, and how likely you are to change your behavior.

Every time the staff washed their hands, they watched the numbers go up on the board. This small incentive motivated the medical staff to wash their hands.

This worked because our brains value immediate rewards over future rewards. Our brains seek out rewards that we can get now, more than the rewards we can get in the future. We all want to be happy, healthy and successful in the future, but the only problem is that the future is so far away.

Our tiny brains can fathom that. So, the here and now you would rather have that margarita and cheese burger now, than something that's uncertain in the future (your health). You're choosing something guaranteed now rather than something that is unknown in the future.

Therefore, in order to bypass this system, we can choose to reward ourselves and others now for behaving in ways that are good for us in the future.

Progress Monitoring

The electronic board the researchers introduced, simply fixated the medical staff attention on improving their performance. The brain does a really good job at this, but it doesn't do such a good job at processing negative information about the future.

What does this mean? This means that if you're trying to get people's attention, you might want to highlight their progress, not their decline. Highlighting their decline can lead to them resenting you. When dealing with people, it's important to keep in mind that you're dealing with emotional creatures.

For example, if you want to stop yourself from smoking cigarettes, you might want to tell yourself:"You know, if I stop smoking, I'll become better at sports." Highlight the progress, not the decline. Giving yourself a sense of control is a really important motivator in changing negative behavior.

Consequently, if you try to get yourself to change a bad behavior, (because the brain is constantly trying to seek ways to control its environment) give yourself a sense of control by highlighting your progress rather than your decline. This response is key to effectively changing anyone's behavior.

Positive Reassurance

Change of behavior is evident with positive reassurance. Only then will you begin to see changes in your behavior and in your habits. If you truly want to motivate change, you might want to rethink how you approach it. At the of the day, fear only impels inaction, while the thrill of a gain impels action.

Highlighting your progress is a sure way to ensure a positive change in behavior. Hence, in order to change behavior in ourselves and in others, we may want to try these positive strategies rather than threats, which ceases us to seek action.

8

SOCIAL MEDIA AND YOUR MENTAL HEALTH

In recent years, social media use has become a widespread epidemic. People just can't seem to get enough of it. As of July 2019, It's estimated that over 4.3 billion people are internet users. Out of the 4.3 billion internet users around the world, 3.5 billion reported having one form of social media platform.

For many of us, logging in and updating our social media accounts has become a daily routine. With the variety of social media platforms now readily available, it's no surprise that 79% of the US population reported having a social media account. That's a staggering 247 million users reported using social media.

To put this in perspective, the total US population is now at 329.3 million. That's almost 80% of the US population. Facebook leads the pack with the highest reported online users. According to a survey conducted by the Pew Research Center, an astonishing 79% of adults reported having a Facebook account. Additionally, 73% reported using YouTube, 32% reported using Instagram, 27% reported using Snapchat and 24% of Americans reported using Twitter. The survey also illustrated that the median American uses three of the eight social media platforms daily. The top three platforms are Facebook, YouTube, and Instagram.

Social media platforms were designed to unite and bring people closer together from all corners of the world. However, with such readily available platforms where anyone can post, tweet, and snap in a matter of seconds. It's not a surprise that social media continues to wreak havoc on every day users. From lack of Self-esteem to cyberbullying, social media can negatively affect your mental health.

Self-esteem

We all have our fair shares of insecurities that we deal with. Whether it's our weight or smile, it's something we learn to cope with. There's nothing wrong with that. However, constantly bombarding yourself with images and videos of other people showing off their luxury, wealth and lifestyle will simply do you no good. It's unhealthy and can impact your self-esteem.

It's easy to get lost in a world where everything is perfect. Where everybody weights a certain weight, drives a certain car and looks a certain way. Where people are always happy and celebrating big accomplishments. Where couples are always laughing and smiling in every post. Where the sun is always bright and shining, a world where the lights keep flashing, and the cameras keep snapping. It's a beautiful world that we all want to be apart off.

The only problem is that it doesn't exist. It's a fantasy world. The sooner you realize this, the better you are off. Trying to appear perfect in a world full of lies will leave you feeling inadequate. After a while, you'll begin to value and seek the opinions of others more than you do your own. This issue can end up affecting your self-esteem, which often leads to depression.

Depression

The link between social media and depression is a widely known fact. When users spend hours viewing and browsing social media platforms, the sudden realization that your life might not be as interesting as others can be daunting. It can make you feel inadequate. Furthermore, social media use has been linked to social isolation and a decreased feeling of satisfaction with life.

Time spent on social media platforms has been shown to increase these feelings. In order to prevent being depressed, set a time limit on social media use. Allocate that time to more meaningful tasks. For example, take time to reevaluate your life and your values.

You can also install apps on your mobile devices that help you feel good about yourself and promote healthy living. You can download meditation apps for starters. Meditating regularly has been linked to helping with depression.

These apps are great and promote positive mindsets and attitudes.

Cyber Bullying

Social media platforms have the ability to instantly connect you to the world. This isn't always a good thing. Being a click away can leave you vulnerable to the unsuspecting world of online bullying. Cyberbullying or cyber harassment is a form of bullying or harassment that takes part online using electronic means. Yes, it's true that teens are more likely than any age group to be the victims of cyberbullying. However, studies show that adults too can be victims of cyberbullying.

It's crucial to understand how the online world works and operates. The terms and conditions differ from that we are accustomed to. With the anonymity of the internet, complete strangers can express their opinions relatively freely. This "protection" afforded by the anonymity allows users online to attack and harass you without physically being present. You could be worlds apart and still be a victim of cyberbullying. So, In order to avoid being a victim of cyberbullying, you must understand that anything you post, tweet or snap is forever engraved into the online database.

Avoid becoming a victim of cyberbullying by taking the time to rethink whatever it is you are posting online. You don't want anything sensitive getting in the wrong hands. Cyberbullying is a real problem that affects millions of users every day. From public embarrassment to sexual harassment, cyberbullying can negatively affect your mental health.

Attention Span

With all the information readily available with a push off a button, it can become difficult to focus. According to a study conducted by Microsoft, the average human being now has an attention span of eight-seconds. This is a sharp decrease from the average attention span of 12 seconds in the year 2000. As time passes, it's only going to get shorter and shorter. With billions of content being viewed, shared and posted every waking minute, it's simply no match for our human brain. As humans, we are always attracted to new and exciting things. Whether that be a new video, song, or a picture, our curiosity gets the best of us. To avoid this, practice mindfulness. Being in their present moment can help improve your attention span.

Interrupts Sleeping Schedule

Having adequate sleep is important to your mental health. A good night of sleep is as essential to survival as water and food. In general, we spend about one-third of our lives sleeping. With the rise of social media, more and more people are finding themselves on their phones late at night.

In a sleep experiment, researchers revealed that those who use social media more than two hours per day were about twice as likely to have disturbed sleep-including decreased sleep quality and difficulty falling asleep-compared to those who use social media 30 minutes per day or less. In a world where the wheels keep turning, and the whistles keep blowing, there are always events taking place around the world. With the fear of missing out on these events, people simply can't stop using social media. Furthermore, a survey of 1,763 adults between the ages of 19–32 showed that people who use social media before bed were one and a half times more likely to experience "disturbed" sleep. Compared to participants who rarely check social media before bed, those who most often check before bed were about 1.5 times more likely to have more disturbed sleep.

With the use of social media gradually becoming the norm in the bedroom, it's not a surprise that people reported having problems falling asleep at night. The brain is also designed to release melatonin at night in order for the body to fall asleep. However, with cellphones and tablets finding their ways in the bedroom late at night, the reflective light produced by such electronic devices keeps the brain activated and alert. The light ends up suppressing the release of melatonin (the hormone our body releases at night in order for us to fall asleep) resulting in sleepless nights. In other words, with the brain on high alert, it makes it difficult to fall asleep.

To prevent this from happening, reduce the amount of time you spend on social media/phone during bed time. Also, it helps if you apply strict rules for yourself. For example, you can make it a rule to limit your use of your cell phone 30 to 50 minutes prior to going to bed. By simply eliminating the use of social media before bed, your brain will thank you with a good night's sleep.

Manage Your Social Media Usage

You don't necessarily have to delete all your social media accounts. In this day and age, we need them to communicate with those around us. It's also a cheap and convenient way to get in touch with those we cherish and love. However, knowing how long you spend on social media platforms is key to understanding the effects they have on your mental health. By limiting your usage, you simply free up space in your busy schedule to do and work on more productive activities. Your brain and the people around you will thank you.

9
REPROGRAM YOUR SUBCONSCIOUS MIND

Whatever the mind can conceive and believe, it can achieve in the physical world. Contrary to popular belief, we become what we think about. Our realities are shaped and formed by the thoughts that occupy our minds. According to the National Science Foundation, it's estimated that the average person has between 12,000 and 60,000 thoughts a day. In addition, 80% of those thoughts are negative and 95% are repetitive thoughts. As a result, we become what we think about. Look around. Your surroundings are the result of your thoughts.

How to change your thought pattern

In order to change your reality, you first have to change your thoughts. People usually seek change by trying to change the outside world. Many have tried and failed. Change has to first occur from the inside before you can see the results outside. In other words, change from within. For example, get to know yourself. What are your likes and dislikes. Study yourself. Study your feelings and emotions. Most people walk around not knowing who they are. They let others dictate who they are instead of showing them.

The problem

One can't expect to change if one doesn't know what it is that needs changing. Let's use a car for an example. When a car suddenly stops operating due to mechanical problems, the first instinct is to figure out what is causing the problem. One typically goes under the hood to assess the situation.

That's where the brains of the car is located. A car cannot run without an engine. It's as good as a toy car that kids get in their cereal boxes.

This is also the same with the human brain. In order to change your thoughts, you have to go under the hood. Booking a flight to Cabo will not change you. It will however change your environment but not you. Your thought patterns will follow you no matter how far you go. It's embedded into your subconscious mind.

There's simply no escaping it. The only logical and reasonable solution, is it come to terms with the fact that we become what we think about. It's as simple as that.

Understanding your thoughts

Learning to understand and see your thoughts in a non judgmental way is one way you can learn to change your reality. By understanding your thoughts, one can finally dictate what enters the mind. Who can do this? Anyone can do this. Each one of us possess the ability to allow or deny any thoughts that crosses our mind. It's an ability that few manage too perfect.

Why? Because it takes time to rewire your subconscious mind. You simply can't expect to change something overnight that took decades to cultivate. Think of it as learning a new language. An individual who has never studied French can't expect to wake up one morning speaking French fluently. It's unheard of. It's the same thing with the subconscious mind. It takes practice and repetition.

Practicing being aware and mindful of your thoughts is one way to reprogram your subconscious mind. Eventually, with practice, you can manage to subconsciously reject any negative thoughts without any effort. As a result, your mind will generate more positive and productive thoughts.

The Mind Is The Most Powerful Tool You Posses

The great philosopher Marcus Aurelius once said a man's life is what his thoughts make of it. Our lives are simply driven and shaped by our minds. Each one of us is in the driver seat of one of the most powerful vessels ever known to mankind. With both hands on the steering wheel, the choice is yours to make. Either let negative thoughts take over your boat and risk going off course. Or, simply grab a hold of your vessel with both hands and redirect it to heights that were previously thought unattainable. A mind set to a definite goal will ultimately achieve that goal. It's inevitable.

∽

10

THE ART OF COMMUNICATING

Communication is the ultimate key to success. One cannot attain success without proper communication skills. Napoleon Hill, best known for his book Think and Grow Rich (which is regarded as one of the best selling self-help books of all time) was once quoted saying, "think twice before you speak, because your words and influence will plant the seed of either success or failure in the mind of another." In other words, be thoughtful of the words you choose to utter. Once they are said, they can only be forgiven not forgotten. This idea is why communication is considered an art.

Even so, communicating effectively is an art anyone can master with practice. There are four main types of communication we use on a daily basis; Verbal, nonverbal, visual and written communication. Communication skills are vital to a healthy and efficient relationship. Often categorized as a "soft skill" or interpersonal skill, communication is the act of sharing information from one person to another person or group of people. We communicate every day in nearly every environment, including in the workplace. Whether you give a slight head nod in agreement or when presenting information to a large group, communication is absolutely necessary when building relationships, sharing ideas, managing a team and much more.

To be an outstanding leader, one has to master the art of communicating his/her thoughts thoroughly and effectively. Developing great communication skills can help you succeed in your career, make you a competitive job candidate and expand your social network. While it may take some time and practice, communication and interpersonal skills are certainly able to be both increased and refined over time.

In this chapter, we take a closer look at the different types of communication and how to strengthen your skills in order to communicate effectively.

Dial up Your Energy When Communicating

Dialing up your energy when communicating makes it easier to have a good time. People tend to mirror the energy level that you put out. If you're coming off as an individual with lower energy, and you start conversing with a coworker, they'll typically mirror your energy and enthusiasm. This response often referred as an emotional contagion in the field of psychology. If you've ever started talking to someone after getting some good news, you'll notice that most times, they ride that high energy wave with you.

So, if you're walking around at a 2/10 energy level all the time, your social interactions are only going to be that, a mere 2/10. When we decide to dial up our energy level to a 6/10, it can feel unnatural and fake at times. Don't sweat it. Commit to it. Our goal isn't to aim for a 10/10 bouncing off the wall type of energy. The goal here is to simply go for a little higher energy than normal.

SOLUTION: If you naturally classify yourself as an introvert, you probably are already aware that the greatest nation in the world is a playing ground for extroverts. With that being said, one doesn't necessarily have to convert to a full blown extrovert, you just have to dial it up a notch. Here are some quick and effective ways to dial up your energy.

Play upbeat music and sing the lyrics at a higher than normal volume. Do 10 push-ups/sit-ups or do several small jumps in place. It may appear crazy from the outside, but it gets me out of my head, into my body and ready to be social.

If you know what you'll be talking about beforehand here's a useful way to help you "dial in" to 6/10 energy: For example, if you have a schedule job interview, here's what you can do to dial up your energy level. Recite your talking points using zero energy. Afterwards, recite your talking points with 100% over the top energy like an infomercial host. When the time comes to present your talking points live, aim for somewhere in the middle.

Be Curious

Being curious will help you be interested in other people. You might be asking yourself, "How can I be interested in other people?" The simple answer? Be curious. Instead of using most of your processing power trying to keep the conversation going, what if you tried focusing on learning one new thing about each person you talk to each day? This response takes your focus from internal (what you're thinking and feeling) to external (I'd better listen to this person so I can learn more about them). With social skills, external is better than internal. You might learn something mundane like, "this person likes basketball," or it could be interesting like "that person collects custom playing cards from around the world."

Solution: At the end of each day, jot down one new thing you've learned about one person. When we work backwards from the end point of "being curious," what does that mean for the rest of the interaction? We have to listen. We have to be focused on the other person to listen. You'll be less focused on yourself (because you'll be focused on the other person).

No One Can Read Your Mind

People have no idea what you're thinking. Not even the slightest clue. And vice versa, you have no idea what they are thinking. You have to effectively communicate whatever it is you're thinking. The worst thing you can do is make an assumption. Making assumptions will rob you of all joy in life. Even if you're not in the mood to communicate, communicating that with others is instrumental to communicating effectively. This mindset can help one elevate their social skills.

Repeat after me: "I cannot read other people's minds. Other people cannot read my mind." This fact is really powerful. If you've ever been in a situation where you think you know what others are thinking about you, and you let those real feeling influence how you behave, then you've experienced this first hand.

Examples Where People Can't Read Your Mind

You walk into a new job, people can't read your mind. You go to a party, people can't read your mind. Also, you walk into a new job, you can't read your new co-worker's mind. You enter a party, you can't read the host's mind. You sit down for a job interview, you can't read your interviewer's mind. Mind reading comes from people's discomfort with the unknown. We as humans WANT to know as much about any situation as we can, and with social situations, we're trying to fit in and not screw up. So, mind reading is a natural tactic we use to reduce that "information gap"

What's the solution? The solution is to simply control only what you can control. If you can't read minds, what else can you do? You walk into a new job. Introduce yourself to as many new people as you can. You enter a party. Say hi to the host and ask them who you should meet at the party. You sit down for a job interview. Since you can't mind read, the best you can do is answer and ask questions about the job, and make small talk with the interviewer. This response also applies after the interaction.

Since mind reading is impossible, you can't think "oh, I bet my new coworker think I'm weird." You can't think "I bet the host thought I was too quiet." You can't think "I bet the interviewer hated me." You can't think these things because you can't mind read.

Solution: If you catch yourself mind reading, gently remind yourself that you can't read minds. You can only control what you can control. (Body language, eye contact, conversation, etc.) Doing this will propel you to heights previously thought unattainable.

The Spotlight Effect Is Real

We all tend to overestimate the amount of focus that other people place on us. It's a phenomenal called the Spotlight Effect. As humans, we tend to place more importance on ourselves in any given social situation. People tend to overestimate the amount that other people notice them. In a 2000 study on The Spotlight Effect, researcher Tom Gilovich and his colleagues found that college students overestimated the percentage of people who noticed the Barry Manilow shirt they were wearing. The Manilow Clad students estimated that 50%

of people would notice their shirt. In fact, only 25% of people noticed Barry. What can we all learn from this? If you have a social slip up, it's not as big of a deal as your mind makes it out to be. Knowing that everyone has at least a little bit of The Spotlight Effect is empowering. This response helps to normalize those feelings of "oh crap, everyone is noticing me."

Action and Solution: If you're in public right now, look up from your phone and see if anyone is paying close attention to you. When you combine this with (no one can read your mind) it becomes liberating. You can start that conversation, or speak up louder than you normally would and the world will not explode, even though it might feel like it.

Perception Vs. Reality

Life is all about perception. It's possible to view the same event two different ways. For example, you say "Hi" to someone but that person doesn't reciprocate but instead brushes past you instead of saying "Hi." There're two possible outcomes you can choose to believe. You can either choose to think positive about the situation or you can choose to think negative. Here's two ways that can unfold.

Option 1, you choose to have a positive view. "They must be preoccupied, they probably didn't hear me." Option 2, you choose to have a negative view. "They don't like me." Let's look at it more in depth:

Scenario 1: You clock in at work, you see your manager and say hi, but she walks right past you without greeting you. Here are two ways you could interpret that event. "Oh no. she must be upset with me. I'd better be careful today." Or instead, you can choose to view this in a more possitive way. For instance, one can say "she might be preoccupied by something. She probably didn't even hear me." Here, we have the same event, you said hello, your manager did not. But we have two options, two lenses we can choose to view the event through. Which option do you think will help you communicate effectively? Obviously, option 2. Here is another example. Scenario 2: You text someone that you're romantically interested in. They don't respond and it's been several hours.

Here are two ways you could interpret that event. "Why didn't they reply?! What did I do?" Or, one can choose an alternative perspective. For example, "They are probably just busy. It likely has nothing to do with me." These are two options for how you view the world. Which option do you think will help you communicate effectively? Again, obviously option 2. Most people default to a negative interpretation of events. This is because humans have a built in negativity bias. Negative things have a greater effect on our psychological state than neutral or positive things.

You can go through your entire day where people compliment you without even thinking about it. But once someone says something negative to you, your entire focus becomes fixated at the negative remark made to you. Your mind will automatically gravitate to that one negative remark that was said to you. It doesn't have to be anything serious. It can be something mundane like a stranger telling you "your shirt sucks."

Solution: When you find yourself making an automatic

negative interpretation of a social event or situation, flip the switch the other way in your mind. Ask yourself: "How could I interpret this differently?" Take 5 minutes and think of one recent situation when you made an automatic negative interpretation. How could you have interpreted that event in a more positive way? This response is a borderline superpower because everything is related.

If you start viewing events through a more positive lens, you'll have better social interactions because people will love being around a positive person. Over time, adopting a positive mindset will filter through everything. You'll start doing this naturally, and it will become your new normal.

First Impressions, Start Before You Open Your Mouth

Turn that frown upside down. Being approachable is key to communicating effectively with others. In order to do this, you have to lose your "resting b*tch face" as it's commonly referred to. In order to lose the "R.B.F," you must learn how to master the "resting happy face." You can practice this by having a slight smile on your face when you're out at an event.

Most people don't realize this, but first impressions start before you ever shake someone's hand or say hi. If you've ever been to a party and someone is laughing and having a great time, and then they happen to meet you, you'll notice that the first impression is already half made before you even meet that person.

They've already set the tone of the interaction by being approachable. What can you do to project this "approachable

WiFi" to people around you? Try using the slight smile when approaching and passing by people. You might feel weird and unnatural when you smile at random people, but this approach works even if you think you look goofy.

Don't worry, that's the spotlight effect messing with your head. The slight smile is a genuine small smile that signals to other people that you are approachable. This response gives off a friendly and approachable vibe to potential friends and partners.

Approachable body language

When your body language is open and approachable, people will have an easier time interacting with you. The sub-message here is, "I want to be here and I want to interact with you. Ways to seem approachable with your body language: Arms uncrossed. Slight smile.

Gesturing with palms open. Palms open, sub-communicates safety. Upright posture while sitting or standing. (pretty much the opposite of being hunched over scrolling on your phone.) All of these stitched together communicate that you have a "positive vibe."

In general, people are going to be more accepting of others who are positive, and to people who add more enjoyment to their lives. Especially at first encounters. So does this mean that you have to be over the top positive 100% of the time? Nope, not at all. If you've struggled with giving off an "approachable vibe" in the past, it might be worth testing a new approach and see if you get different results.

Solution: The next time you're in a social situation (could be at work, a party, school, etc.) test out the slight smile and approachable body language. You'll gradually but surely come to the conclusion that conversations are a little easier to start when you are already smiling.

11

THE ART OF COMMUNICATING: PART 2

If you classify yourself as an extrovert, small talk is a walk in the park. For those that classify themselves as introverts, engaging in small talk can be tiresome. But if one is truly dedicated to bettering themselves, mastering the art of small talk can take you a long way. It's essential and helps you move from lighter topics to deeper topics so that you can build rapport. Think of it as boiling cold water on a stove. When you turn on the stove to boil water, it takes a few minutes for the water to heat up enough to start boiling. People will think things like: "men, I HATE small talk, I prefer having a deeper conversation!" They are missing the point of small talk.

Small Talk Is Necessary

Small talk is getting you to a place where you CAN go deeper. Not only does small talk have a point, it's a crucial basis for building rapport. Let's say your goal is making new friends at a new job. Here's what that process might look like. This may happen over a span of a few weeks or months. Introduce yourself to coworker > make small talk > build rapport > deeper conversation > make plans to meet up outside of work. You may need to make small talk several times over a few weeks. Then, rapport develops and deeper topics can be introduced. Those deeper topics can come up easily because of all the small talk you've had before that point.

Systems Beat Goals

Communicating effectively is a goal. Making small talk with people in your life is a system. A goal is a destination on a map. A system is a car that will get you to that goal. I'm willing to bet that MOST people who are friends with people started out by making small talk with them first. If you make an effort to make more small talk, you'll have more people in your life who are "on the road" to being friends with you.

Solution: If you're someone who usually avoids small talk, take the initiative and make small talk with 3 people in your life this week that you normally wouldn't have. This can be someone at work, the person sitting behind you in class, a complete stranger passing you by on the streets or the clerk at the counter. The objective here isn't to get any specific outcome, the objective is simply to do it. If you've made their day 1% better, great!

Try Not To Interrupt

If you accidentally interrupt, say "you were saying..." and

bring up the last thing they said to get them back on track. This response shows that you were listening. No one likes to be interrupted. It sucks. But hey, it's bound to happen from time to time. Maybe your friend brings up something that you know a lot about, and you interject because you're really excited to add to the conversation.

I know your interruption was coming from a great place, but this disrupts the flow of things. Here's what you can say to get back on track and show the other person that you were listening, not just waiting for your turn to speak: "Before I interrupted you, you were saying....? "This phrase is gold because it demonstrates two things: one, it acknowledges that you interrupted, and it shows that you were listening. (listening so well that you can provide them a jumping off point to get back to what they were saying.)

Two, if you are the one who gets interrupted, it's actually a good thing. Let them finish their thought and then say: "going back to what I was saying about..." This response is subtle and professional. You're not calling them out, you're just doing a little conversational nudge. If they get the hint, great! If not, rinse and repeat.

Solution: If you accidentally interrupt someone, say "Before I interrupted you, you were saying...? "to help them get back on track. If you get interrupted, say, "Going back to what I was saying about..." to get yourself back on track.

LISTEN, Listen And Listen Some More

Make it a habit to give whoever you are with the gift of your attention. Listening is a skill that anyone can acquire, but it takes patience and practice to cultivate. When engaging in conversations, make it an effort to listen. Try to absorb as much information as you can. Afterwards, try to come up with observations and questions that show that you were 100 percent engaged in the conversation.

Channel your inner talk show when communicating with others. Good talk show hosts make their guests look good. They are curious about their guests. Listen well. Ask great questions. Make insightful observations. When we approach conversations with the Talk Show Host Mindset, our focus isn't on our internal state, our thoughts, our feelings, etc.

Our focus is on the other person. And showing that kind of presence is increasingly rare, especially in the age of smartphones. Most people spring load their response. They already know what they'll respond with before the other person is even done talking. Big mistake. If you do this, you're communicating "I'm not listening to you." If they bring up something that they've experienced, it's typically a good idea to ask them a question about it, or make an observation about it. Don't try to up one them with your story. Save your story for another day.

Example: "So after I graduated from UCLA, I decided to pack up some of my things, sold the rest of my belongings, and moved to New York." There's so many possible options to comment on! What did you study at UCLA? It must have been hard to pick up and go like that…what was the moment you decided to move like? How long have you been in NY for?

Wow, you're really brave! I don't think I could have done that... I've been to New York for New Years, it was breathtaking... All these responses demonstrate that you were engaged and listening to what they were saying.

Solution: Next time you're in a conversation, channel your inner talk show host mindset by being curious and interested in the other person. When possible, bring up questions/observations that relate to what they've said. If you notice that the other person is mirroring your body language, that's a great sign! This response means that you two are in rapport and connecting. You can also trigger this by mirroring them first.

If you've ever been talking to someone and thought: "I wonder if this person is enjoying our conversation?" All you have to do is use the Mirror Test. When we are "in rapport" with someone, we naturally mirror our body language, and even our breathing. How can you use this to tell if you're connecting with your conversational partner?

Examples Of Mirroring

When one person takes a drink, the other one does too. When one person leans against the bar, the other one does as well. When one person smiles, the other one does too. If you two aren't naturally mirroring yet, begin the mirroring: When they take a drink, you take one too. When they lean against the bar, you do too. When they smile, you smile too. Then, after mirroring them for a bit, notice how they start to mirror you when you drink, lean, or smile. We tend to like and trust people who are similar to us, and mirroring body language is a great way to trigger liking and trust.

Solution: Use the Mirror Test while making small talk to see if you're in rapport with your conversational partner.

The Three F's

If you remember something "cringey" you did in the past, try applying the 3 F's method. Flush, Fix and Forget.

Flush: Take a breath and get some emotional distance from that memory. Fix: Is there anything you can change next time? Forget: Give yourself permission to forget it.

Have you ever told a joke to someone and they didn't get your joke? I have, and I later replayed the conversation in my head on a loop. Worse than that, you may have started to associate that interaction into who you are, and associate it with your identity. Not good, here is how to fix that.

How To Apply The Three F's

Realize that this type of negative over generalization of events is a form of cognitive distortion known as "labeling." Labeling is insidious because it fuses actions, which are tiny sample sizes of behavior, with our identity. Author and researcher, Brené Brown has a philosophy: Guilt = I did a bad thing. Shame = I AM a bad person. Once we separate our actions from our identity, we become free. So, the next time you do something awkward:

Flush it. Destroy the link between your actions and who you are. Delete all thoughts of "What do these actions say about who I am as a person?" Imagine that you are watching yourself in the 3rd person doing the embarrassing thing, this idea will help you get some emotional distance. Fix it. If there is anything about the situation that is within your control, mentally adjust your approach next time. Forget it. Move on. Close the book. Replaying an event is counterproductive and will almost certainly lead to "because that's who I am" thinking. Often, the biggest key here is simply giving yourself permission to move on. There are things you can control, and things you can't. The past falls into the "I can't control category."

Solution: Use Flush, Fix, and Forget next time you remember something awkward you did in the past, or you do something awkward in the future and you need to rapidly correct course. Once you do this a few times, you'll be shocked at how rapidly you can move from Flush through Fix to Forget. You'll be able to do this in the moment, and rapidly rebound from awkward moments almost in real time. This idea is definitely a super power most people forget to apply and use.

Body Language Communicates More Than The Words That Are Coming Out Of Your Mouth

In most cases, people could take up more space, gesture more with their hands and stop fidgeting. These signal to others that you're comfortable with yourself. Which helps them feel comfortable too.

The three thing I consistently see with people who are confident and relaxed in social situations is;

- **Confident People Are Not Afraid To Take Up Space:** This means that they might drape their arm over the empty chair next to them. They won't default to crossing their arms or legs. (Collapsed body language) They'll keep their hands out of their pockets. The mindset here is: "I deserve to take up space in the world."

- **Confident People gesture more with their hands:** Gestures help make your stories, jokes, or small talk more engaging. If you've ever struggled with being higher energy, or showing enthusiasm, gesturing a bit more will help. This also helps with taking up more space.

- **Confident People don't fidget much or at all**: If you're a chronic fidgeter try this: focus all your fidgeting to your toes. (When I first read about this, I thought it was crazy.) That's right, wiggle your toes in your shoes, this response will help you feel more present in the moment.

Relax, Take Up Space And Be Comfortable

If you're taking up space, gesturing more, and not fidgeting, it's sending the "Social WI-FI" that you're comfortable doing whatever you're doing. It could be making small talk at a party, giving a presentation at work, or getting to know someone on a first date.

The more comfortable you appear, the more comfortable other people will feel as a result. Solution: Take up more space, gesture more, fidget with your toes, and internalize the mindset of "I deserve to take up space in the world."

Prep A Quick Summation/Story Of Your Day/Weekend

People will ask, have something ready. Many people who struggle with their mind going blank may not realize that a little prep can go a long way.

Craft a quick summary of your day or weekend, or a recent event. I used to be caught off guard when someone would ask me "What have you been up to lately?" "Not much." Would be my default response. It can't get less compelling than that.

Now, I take 2 minutes before a social event and I ask myself; "What is one mildly interesting thing I've done lately?"

By doing this little exercise, I have an interesting conversation topic to bring up when someone asks me what I've been up to, rather than responding with the usual "Not much.."

Note: If you haven't been doing anything new or interesting, it may be time to shake up your routine a little. Big bonus points if you can deliver that quick summation in a story format. Studies show that people are more likely to listen to you if you are a good at telling stories.

How to craft a compelling story:

With stories, details don't matter. Better to focus on painting a picture inside someone's mind.

- Who are the people in the story?
- Where? Set the scene
- Encounter the obstacle

- Overcome the obstacle
- Resolution

Your quick summary or story doesn't have to be anything big. It can be about getting supplies from your local Home Depot, going out to of lunch and/or anything similar. If you provide people with something mildly interesting to grab on too, they will. This idea can lead to having an interesting conversation.

Solution: Sit down and think of 1–2 things you've done recently that you can bring up the next time someone asks you what you've been up to.

Laying Boundaries Is Important

People will treat you however you let them. Hard to know if people are stepping over boundaries if you aren't sure what those boundaries are. Here is a great example of crafting boundaries.

Isaiah moves into a new apartment and invites friends/family over for a housewarming party. He makes it known that he would like everyone to leave their shoes by the door before entering the apartment. Shortly after people start showing up, some people ignore the request and proceed to enter the apartment with their shoes on. "We never took our shoes off in your old apartment" they said.

Isaiah tells them again "I don't do shoes in my apartment. Please remove your shoes and place them by the door." After a few weeks, friends and family get the message. "Isaiah doesn't do shoes in his apartment."

Isaiah was assertive in a respectful way, and as a result, he trained people to remove their shoes before entering his apartment instead of allowing friends/family to override his boundaries. (Better for him, better for them).

Saying No Is A Crucial Communication Skill

Again, people will treat you however you let them. Over time, people will mistake your kindness for weakness. You'll suffer greatly if you have a hard time telling people no. Here is my personal framework for being assertive and saying no.

Step 1: Know your boundaries. It's really hard to know if people are stepping over your boundaries if you're not clear on what those boundaries are. Here are my boundaries.

- **Time:** I value my time above all else. I expect myself and people in my life to respect all scheduled events.

- **Communication:** I value respectful communication. I expect myself and the people in my life to communicate in a respectful way.

- **Follow Through:** Your word is your bond. I value people who follow through on their promises. If someone in my life commits to do something, I expect them to be liable to their word and follow through on their promise.

If people push the boundaries of time, communication, and follow-through, I know it's either time for a tough conversation, or it's time to part ways. Holding grudges does nothing for you but fill your heart with hatred and resentment.

Obviously, this can be very nuanced. If your boss pushes your boundaries, you can't exactly walk out the door that day. But it is worth having a conversation with them about creating the best work environment you can. If they aren't up for that, there are plenty of jobs out there with better bosses, I promise you. Everyone's personal boundaries will vary.

Step 2: Saying "No" when people step over those boundaries.

IF SOMEONE STEPS over your personal boundaries, it's fine to say no. Often, you'll need to give them a reason why you're saying no to their request. **For example:** Your manager gives you work over the weekend. You could say: "Hey (managers name), unfortunately I'm not going to be able to get you the project by the date requested because it would mean that I would have to put in hours over the weekend. I've already committed that weekend time to my family/spouse/hobbies, and I want to follow through for them."

I could get the project done for you early next week, or we can schedule a time to talk more about the details and scheduling before I start." You stuck with your plans and followed through.

For example: A friend asks you to give them a ride to the airport with short notice. Here's what one can say to that request. "Hey, I'm not going to be able to give you a ride to the airport tomorrow because I already have my day planned out and I won't be able to change my day around with such short notice."

NOTE: Some people might play the "guilt" card on you. This response is fine. If they say something like "Well, I guess I'll walk home from the airport then, thanks anyway." Take a moment before you respond and consider these two things,: Good friends don't guilt trip other friends. If they do, you can respond with something like this:

"I believe that you're smart and capable of getting from the airport to your house. I have 100% faith in you. I'd love to help, but I can't change my entire day on such short notice."

It's okay to restate your no, if they push it, and sometimes people will push it, believe me when I tell you this. Through your actions, you're always training people on how to treat you. If you say yes to a lot of stuff that makes your life less fun and ignore your needs, you're training people in your life that putting stuff on your plate is acceptable to you.

Solution: Start exercising your "**No**" muscles. Say no to one thing (big or small) this week that you might have automatically said yes to. Come up with your own personal boundaries. What's important to you? What do you expect out of yourself and others?

Saying "Yes" Is Important Too

Don't say yes to things you don't want to do, but say yes to new or exciting experiences and opportunities. What if you flipped your default from "no" to "yes" for one week? This response means instead of talking yourself out of events, you talk yourself into doing things that you'll remember forever.

I call this the yes I can mindset. For one week, apply the "Yes" mindset. Say yes when… a friend asks you to go to the movies at 6 P.M in the evening even though you have work the next day. A classmate asks you to join their study group. You see a networking event that you'd normally talk yourself out of. You get asked to go on a hike/run with only an hour notice, yes I can!

YES I Can!

This "yes I can" mindset is all about you saying yes to yourself and yes to opportunities that you might turn down. Picture a circle,… my theory is that the more we say yes, or no to things over time, the more the circle expands or contracts. If you say no most of the time, the circle becomes almost non existent. If you consistently decline invites, eventually they stop coming because people assume you'll say no.

But, if you strategically default to yes, you'll notice that circle grow. You'll expand your comfort zone, meet new people, have new experiences. The great thing about the "yes I can" is that you can dial it up or down based on how social you want to be.

Solution: For one week, apply the "Yes I Can" mindset. Say yes to one eventuality that you'd normally say no to out of reflect.

Notable Mentions

- If you're arguing, you've already lost. If you take the time to stop and try to understand the other person's perspective as best you can first, you might be able to avoid the argument.

- Confidence comes from competence. Everyone has at least one thing that they are good at. Remembering that one thing before being social can make you feel more confident in the moment.

- "Be yourself" is misinterpreted advice. Your ultimate goal should be to Improve and better yourself overtime. Always place your best foot forward each and every day. Working on your communication/people skills does not make you fake.

- Life is fluid and forever evolving. If you start acting more confident, the world will accept that new version of you. Over time, that becomes your new normal.

- Be conscious and observant of the comments people around you make as you better yourself. Those who make quirky remarks such as "I liked the old you better" are likely not a right fit for you. Don't be afraid to part ways with them, your success depends on it.

12

MIND OVER MATTER

We're usually quick to point out our haters but never stop to think to do the same with ourselves. As conscious beings, we spent the better part of our lives constantly bombarding our minds with self talk. Almost all of them are constructive and negative. We talk to ourselves in a way that we would never allow another person to speak to us.

It's a continuous cycle that goes on and on. To a point where one starts believing in his/her skeptical thoughts. The truth is, the biggest enemy you have to deal with is yourself. We are the creators and destroyers of our realities. Each one of us is here today because of the thoughts we let occupy our minds. When it comes to our past mistakes and failures, we tend to be our own judge, jury and executioner.

The Biggest Enemy You'll Ever Have To Deal With Is Yourself ~

We analyze and scrutinize our smallest mistakes over and over while ignoring all that we have achieved. It's as if we magnify all our failures and down play all our accomplishments. We focus too much time and energy worrying, doubting and trying to live up to the expectations of others that we end up forgetting and neglecting ourselves. Anxiously waiting for the perfect moment to act on our dreams.

Why? Because it's easier to sit back and hope things get better than it is to set the bar high and risk failing. We are so scared to fail at the things we love and enjoy that we end up settling for a mediocre life. The truth is, no one truly knows what you are capable of doing, not even you. Until you do it.

There's no perfect time or a perfect moment to do something. Act now. When self doubt creeps in, you MUST call it out and defend your values. Don't judge it. Acknowledge it and let it pass. Over time, you'll realize that the only "hater" that was holding you back was YOU. "The only limitation is that which one sets up in one's own mind" — Napoleon Hill.

13

THE 21/90 RULE

How long does it take to form a habit? Or better yet, how long does it take for one to turn a habit to a lifestyle? These questions are often asked by people who want to acquire and form healthy habits. To investigate the process of habit formation in everyday life, an experiment was conducted by the University Of London to research and understand how habits are formed. The experiment was conducted on 96 volunteers, who were given the option to either choose an eating, drinking, or activity behavior to carry out daily in the same context for three months.

The participants were instructed to record their doings daily on a website, which tracked and monitored the individual's progress. The majority (82) of participants provided sufficient data for analysis, and increases in the automaticity were examined over the study duration. Performing the behavior more consistently was associated with a better model fit. Surprisingly enough, that data revealed that the time it took participants to reach 95% off their asymptote of automaticity ranged from 18 to 254 days; indicating considerable variation in how long it takes people to reach their limit of automaticity. Additionally, the act of missing a day does not hinder or affect the habit formation process. With repetition of a behavior in a persistent context, automaticity increases following an asymptotic curve was modeled at the individual level.

Planning

Performing an action for the first time requires planning, even if plans are formed only moments before the action is performed. All participants had to schedule and register their activity progress online. As behaviors are repeated in consistent settings, they begin to move more efficiently and with less thought as control of the behavior transfers too cues in the environment that activate an automatic response.

The Experiment

The experiment was conducted on college students. Researchers sent out flyers to students via the university's email. Interested participants responded by attending an individual meeting, of whom 96 chose to participate in the study. For those who agreed to participate for the entire duration of the experiment (12 weeks), a payment of 30 pounds was offered to each participant.

The 96 participants (30 men, 66 women) were predominantly postgraduate students (two were undergraduates) with a mean age of 27 (range 21—45). The majority (65%) were White and born in the UK or Europe. In the end, 27 of the participants chose an eating behavior, 31 chose a drinking behavior (water), 34 chose an exercise behavior and four of the remaining participants chose meditation.

Analysis

The hypothesis in this study was that repeating a behavior would result in increasing automaticity scores, which would follow an asymptotic curve. To test this hypothesis, researchers plotted each individual's daily automaticity scores over 12 weeks to examine the shape of the individual automaticity curves, and examined the fit of an asymptotic curve.

To identify commonalities across individuals, researchers calculated the time taken for automaticity scores to plateau and the level of automaticity at the plateau. Ideally, they would have looked at the relationship between the number of repetitions and automaticity, but because not all participants logged on to the website every day, there were days for which behavioral data were unavailable.

Consequently, they examined the relationship between the day of the study and automaticity and considered consistency of performance as a separate predictor. The first (number of reported repetitions) was calculated by simply summing all the occasions when a participant reported that they had performed the behavior. The second (percent compliance) was calculated as the percentage of all days for which data were reported that the participant reported having performed the behavior.

Results

When it was all set and done, 14 participants did not enter data. Habit formation beyond day 60 and were considered to have dropped out of the study.

The remaining 82 participants logged on an average (median) off 47 out of 84 days, as well as the occasions on which they entered behavior data retrospectively, this event gave an average of 76 days for which data were available.

As a result, researchers discovered that, out of the 82 remaining participants, it took an average of 21 days for participants to set up a habit and an average of 90 days for them to make it a permanent lifestyle change.

How To Apply The 21/90 Rule

In order for one to effectively apply the 21/90 rule, one must first decide what they want to accomplish/change. This item could be a personal or professional goal.

Jot it down in your journal or on your phone/laptop. Whatever method you decide to use, make sure it is visible to you.

Don't be afraid of starting from the beginning, everyone has a different starting point and a different destination. Focus on you and your goals.

The rest will fall in place accordingly. So, in order to mold your daily habits into a lifestyle, simply incorporate the 21/90 rule in your daily routine.

Commit to your goals for 21 days and they'll become a habit. Commit to your goals for 90 days and they will become a part of your lifestyle.

14

FEAR: FALSE EVIDENCE APPEARING REAL

As humans, we have a tendency to fear things. We spend so much time pondering on the "what ifs" moments in life that we forget to live in the present moment. As mortal beings, it's the price we have to pay. We are only gifted this one opportunity to live our lives. It's like writing, casting, directing and editing your own blockbuster film. It's a great opportunity that offers joy in abundance.

The only downside is once the film is shot, the scene continues with or without you. New actors are born and life goes on. Consequently, we spend that time worrying about things that will never happen to us while stressing the things that are predestined to happen to us. You can choose to live and go through life as it unfolds. Fear is simply a misuse of the creative imagination that has been placed in each of us. Since we are all smart and creative, we imagine all the things that could happen, that might happen, that will happen, or if this or that happens. Nothing in life is meant to be feared, it is only meant to be understood. Now is the time to understand more, so that you may fear less.

- **Fear of Poverty:** The fear of poverty hinders a lot of people from achieving their goals. Just the thought of it makes me cringe. However, by letting go of the fear of poverty, one can quickly come to the realization that life unfolds one day at a time. Success doesn't happen overnight. The process takes time and patience. Don't let the fear of poverty stunt and hinder your growth to success.

- **Fear Of Criticism:** No one likes getting criticized, especially by close friends and family members. It makes one feel inadequate. As captains and rulers of our own ships, we're right 10 out of 9 times. Anything said that doesn't sit well with us doesn't make it onboard. It's the way our brains operate. We fear being singled out and scrutinized. It's uncomfortable. We let emotions get in the way. However, people are always going to have something to say. The way one chooses to handle and interpret criticism is the key to understanding and overcoming the fear of criticism. Keep in mind that opinions are one of the cheapest commodities on earth. Everyone has one, but only one counts, yours.

- **Fear Of Ill Health:** The fear of ill health is crippling. From the common cold to life threatening symptoms, the fear of ill health is always hovering around our minds. Not being able to freely operate your body mentally or physically can cause one inner pain and resentment. The local hospitals are filled with people who go through such experiences daily.

- **Fear Of Lost Of Love:** Finding someone to fall in love with is not an easy task. It usually takes a couple hundred million things to align for it to even be possible. That's why falling in love is such a beautiful thing. It's a rollercoaster ride like no other. However, lost of love from a loved one is second to none. Especially in romantic relationships, where things can escalate quickly. Usually, driven by deep emotions and fueled by self doubt, it often results in self loathing, depression, Anxiety and suicide in extreme situations. That's why it's crucial for one to accept and understand the fear of loss of love. Everyone you meet is not destined to be in your life forever. Some people stop by while others check in for an extended stay. It's just the way it is. At the end of the day, the ones that are meant to be, will be.

- **Fear Of Old Age:** Too many, being old is synonymous with the inability to move freely. It's a fear like no other. But, being old should be viewed as blessing. Not too many people make it too "old age." It's an experience too many people miss out on. It's a wonderful stage in the process of life. It's a stage filled with love and knowledge. A stage where one can reflect on life experiences and lessons. Becoming old shouldn't be feared. It should be excepted. By understanding and accepting the fear of old age, one can live to see and appreciate the present moment.

- **Fear Of Death:** Fear Of Death: Like any other story, there's a beginning, a middle and an end. Life's no different. For example, some people live to be 100, while others barely make it to their first birthdays. It's a fact. It happens to all living organisms on this planet. It's often referred to as the "process of life." As a result, no matter where you are in the process, accepting and understanding death is key to living. You never know when your time will be up. Accept death and free yourself from constant worry. Norman Cousins, a world peace advocate once said, death is not the greatest loss in life. The greatest loss is what dies inside us while we live.

15

OVERCOME FEAR AND BUILD CONFIDENCE

People mean well when they say, "It's only in your head. Don't worry. There's nothing to be afraid of." Although such remarks may relief fear in the present moment, in the long run, it doesn't build confidence nor cure fear. Yes, fear is real. As real as the words you are reading right now. This idea is a fact not a matter of opinion. In order to conquer fear, one must first acknowledge it's existence before trying to conquer it. Attempting to conquer fear before acknowledging its existence is ineffective.

Fear is mental, meaning it's a psychological problem. Fear such as embarrassment, tension, anxiety, and panic, all stem from mismanaged negative thoughts. But simply knowing the breeding ground of fear doesn't cure it at all. However, knowing the breeding ground puts one in a position to conquer it. As we all know, fear stunts and hinders a lot of people of reaching their true potential. The number one enemy of success is fear. Fear stops people from capitalizing on life changing opportunities, fear wears down your momentum, fear makes people sick, causes pain, shortens life, fear even closes your mouth when you want to talk.

Fear and uncertainty explains why we still have economic recessions in this day and age. Fear explains why millions of people accomplish little and enjoy little. Truly, fear is a powerful force. A force that if left unchecked could potentially be detrimental to your success. In one way or another, fear prevents people from getting what they want from life. Fear of all kinds and sizes is a form of psychological infection. We can cure a mental infection the same way we cure a body infection, with specified treatment.

The cure of fear is taking action. Indecision and procrastination, on the other hand, breeds fear. You have to condition yourself that all fear and confidence is acquired and developed. No one is born with fear or confidence. Those you know who radiate confidence, who have conquered worry, who are at ease everywhere and at all the times, acquired every bit of their confidence. And guess what? You can too.

Build Confidence And Destroy Fear

When faced with a tough predicament, most people hope for solution. Hope is a start, but hope alone needs action to be effective. Next time you experience fear, calm yourself, then search for an answer to this question: "What kind of action can I take to conquer my fear? First, isolate your fear. Determine exactly what you are afraid of. Then take action. There's an action for any kind of fear. Remember, hesitation only enlarges and magnifies the fear. Take action promptly. Be decisive. Much lack of self confidence can be traced directly to fear.

Your Mind Is Your Bank

In order for one to buy anything of significant value such as a house, a car, or a new business, one has to have "good credit" in order to be approved for a bank loan. Same goes with your brain. In order to start thinking more positively, one has to deposit only positive thoughts in their memory bank. It's just like a line of credit, you have to gradually build it from the ground up. It doesn't just happen over night, it's going to take time.

Everyone encounters innumerable of unpleasant, embarrassing, and discouraging thoughts every day. Unsuccessful and successful people deal with these situations in total opposite ways. Unsuccessful people take them to heart. They make it a personal matter. They dwell on the unpleasant situations, relieving it in a constant loop. Depositing negative thoughts in their memory bank.

Confident, successful people on the other hand, don't give it another thought. Successful people specialize in putting positive thoughts into their memory bank. Negative, unpleasant thoughts deposited in your mind affect your mind the same way. Negative thoughts produce needless wear and tear on your brain. They create worry, frustration, and feelings of Inferiority and inadequacy. Practice depositing good thoughts in your memory bank. This place boosts confidence and squashes fear. It gives you that feel good feeling.

Thought Deposits

Our brains are wired like a bank. Every day, you make thought deposits in your "mind bank." These thoughts deposits grow and become your memory. When you settle down to think or when you face a problem, in effect you say to your memory bank, "what do I already know about this?" Your memory bank automatically answers and supplies you with bits of information relating the too said situation that you deposited on previous occasions.

Your memory, in this scenario, is the supplier of materials for your new thoughts. The teller in your memory bank is tremendously reliable. He never forgets. If you approach him and say; "Mr. Teller, let me withdraw some thoughts I deposited in the past proving I'm a failure." Again, Mr. Teller says sure, remember how you failed in the past when you opened that new business?

Remember what your high school math teacher once told you, that you'll never amount to anything… remember that one time you overheard, your friends/family/co-workers say about you … Remember… and on and on, curving out every square inch of your brain to prove you are inadequate.

But suppose you visit your memory teller with a more positive request. "Mr. Teller, I face a dire situation. Can you please supply me with any thoughts that will give me reassurance and confidence in myself?" And again, Mr. Teller says, sure, but this time, he delivers thoughts you deposited earlier that say you can follow.

Thoughts you once had as a child to be and do all that your heart desired. Thoughts of great success and achievements, thoughts such as; remember the wonderful job you did in a similar situation.... remember how much confidence your high school teacher instilled in you.... remember the good things your friends/family/co-workers said about you ... Mr. Teller lets you withdraw the thoughts you want to withdraw. Make it a habit to only withdraw positive thoughts.

Stop Committing Mental And Spiritual Suicide

In order to stop committing mental and spiritual suicide, one has to first stop drawing negative thoughts from their memory bank. Refrain from building mental monsters. Refuse to withdraw the unpleasant thoughts from your memory bank. When you remember a situation of any kind, concentrate on the good part of the experience, no matter what the memory or circumstance, focus on the good. If you find yourself thinking about the negative side, turn your mind off. Your mind wants you to forget the unpleasant. If you will only cooperate, unpleasant memories will slowly disperse.

Let them fade away. Act the way you want to feel. Action cures fear. Isolate your fear and then take a constructive action. Inaction (doing nothing about a situation) strengthens fear and destroys confidence. Don't let negative, self loathing thoughts grow into mental monsters. Simply refuse to recollect unpleasant events or situations. Make it a habit to deposit and withdraw only positive thoughts in your memory bank. Over time, your confidence, that feeling of being on top of the world, will gradually rise again.

How To Build Your Thought Credit

Here is a great plan to help build your thought credit. After waking up in the morning and before going to bed each night, deposit at least one good thought in your memory bank. Count your blessings. Be grateful of all the good in your life.

Recall the many good things you have to be thankful for; your wife, husband, children, pets, friends, family, health etc. Recall the good things you saw people do today. Recall your little victories and accomplishments. Go over the reasons why you are glad to be alive.

A person can make a mental monster out of any unpleasant situation. For example, a job loss, a failed romantic relationship, or even a bad business investment.

It's clear that any negative thought, big or small, if fertilized with repeated recall, can develop into a real mind monster, breaking down confidence and paving the way to serious psychological pain and suffering. Avoid depositing negative thoughts in your memory bank. Make it a habit to only withdraw and deposit positive thoughts from and into your memory bank.

16
FAILURE IS BOUND TO HAPPEN

One moment, you're at the top of the world, living care free with no doubt in sight. Casually minding your business, as you go on with your affairs. Then suddenly, out of nowhere, life strikes back unannounced. You find yourself drowning in self doubt and resentment. Aimlessly going through life without a definite plan or a purpose. Patiently waiting and hoping someone comes around and saves you. Wishing life was easier.

This is the mindset of failure. When you fail, bear in mind that every failure, every adversity, and every heartache carries with it the seed of an equal or greater benefit. So don't wish your life was easier, wish you were better. Failure is simply a few errors in judgment repeated constantly. In life, anything worth doing is worth doing poorly at first until you can learn to do it well.

How To Bounce Back

Focus on you. Focusing on oneself is a difficult habit to cultivate. It takes discipline and self control to ensure that one is not wasting valuable time on miscellaneous tasks. Prioritizing your own needs over others is the ultimate key to learning how to focus on yourself. As ruthless as it may sound, it's the only way to guarantee you don't waste valuable time on people who don't reciprocate.

Don't Play the Blame Game

The victim mindset drastically dilutes the human potential. You've to take full personal responsibility of your past and your current circumstances. Read the following phrase aloud; from now on, I will accept and take full responsibility for my past and mistakes. I understand that the beginning of wisdom is to accept and to acknowledge the responsibility for my own problems and that by accepting responsibility for my past, I free myself to move into a bigger, brighter future of my own choosing.

The bad news is that the past was in your hands, but the great news is that the future is also in your hands. So, own up to your faults and failures. It's the only way one can move forward with the future. Wasting valuable time blaming others does nothing but create more problems. Own up to your mistakes and move on. Acknowledging and accepting your faults when you are in the wrong is a sign of maturity. Blaming others for your own past mistakes and mishaps is not.

Choose Optimism

In every situation, make it a habit to expect the best, prepare for the worst and capitalize on what comes. Make it a habit to find the good in the bad. In any given situation, no matter how bad the circumstances might seem at the time. You MUST train your subconscious mind to find the good in all aspects of your life. It doesn't matter if you lost your job, are living on the streets, going through a divorce or lost a loved one. There's always something good one can take away from any dire situation.

Be Open to Alternatives

Sometimes, blessings come in disguises. Say you didn't get the job you wanted. Don't be afraid to go another route. It could ultimately lead you to your dream job faster than the previously thought route. Being open to alternatives simply keeps doors open and windows ajar at all times. Don't fear the unknown. Instead, embrace it. It can undoubtedly change one's life for the better.

Be Gentle With Yourself

As I have previously said before, we can be too hard on ourselves. When it comes to our past mistakes and failures, we tend to be our own judge, jury and executioner. We analyze and scrutinize our smallest mistakes over and over while ignoring all that we have achieved. As thinking beings, we strive for the best. And why not? Who doesn't like to win? But sometimes, we can take things a little too far. We tend to set the bar so high that the only cushion we have to fall back on tends to be failure and defeat. Remember, pace yourself. Set smaller goals to help boost your self confidence. Slow and steady wins the race.

Ask For Help

Pride is defined by the Webster dictionary as "The quality or state of being proud; inordinate self-esteem; an unreasonable conceit of one's own superiority in talents, beauty, wealth, rank, etc., which manifests itself in lofty airs, distance, reserve, and often in contempt of others. Pride is a beautiful word in disguise. A sheep in wolf clothing so to speak. However, when one dissects the word you'll quickly come to an understanding that only fools have pride. DON'T BE A FOOL. Put your pride in the back burner. Seek help when in need. Don't be macho. It can save and help you mature into the person you always envisioned your self being. It may be hard at first, but keep in mind the benefits you set to reap and gain after you seek help.

Winners Never Quit!

You were born to win, but to be a winner, you must plan to win, prepare to win, and expect to win. Failure is bound to happen. If you don't succeed at first, try, try and try again. Accept these terms and keep trying. It's not just a saying, it's a lifestyle. You must be willing to go again and again until you can't go any longer. And when you think you can't go any longer, you have to dig deeper and deeper until you get the strength to keep on going.

One cannot take NO for a final answer. Instead, analyze your mistakes and draw up a new game plan. Conquering and understanding failure is one way to achieve success. You have to know what doesn't work in order to identify what does. It's a process that requires a little bit of faith and persistence. Once you understand this, the world becomes your oyster. You'll eventually find yourself in a position to indulge in all the Wonderfull opportunities life has to offer. "Our greatest glory is not in never falling, but in rising every time we fall" - Confucius.

17

SELF DISCIPLINE

Of all the topics we've covered thus far, none is more important than self discipline. Discipline is the bridge between failure and success. It takes self discipline to master setting goals, to be a great leader, to communicate effectively with others, to conquer procrastination and to turn new habits into a lifestyle. If you don't make self discipline a part of your daily life, the results you seek will be inconsistent.

The lack of self discipline is the number one reason millions of people around the world continue to fall short of their goals, even after possessing and acquiring all the knowledge and experiences one could possibly attain. Without self discipline, we find ourselves aimlessly wandering through life, settling, rather than striving to become the best versions of ourselves. For the most part, we tend to choose today's pleasure rather than tomorrow's fortune.

It Takes Discipline To Change

For every disciplined effort, there is a constant reward. It takes discipline to sufficiently manage and allocate your time. It takes discipline to silent the critic in your head. It takes discipline to conquer fear, failure, poverty, criticism, and worry. It takes discipline to keep going when the nagging voice within us brings up the possibility of failure. It takes discipline to admit your mistakes, it takes discipline to recognize the limitations you set for yourself.

It takes discipline to silent the voice of the human ego. It takes discipline to be transparent with yourself and with others. It takes discipline to change a bad habit. It takes discipline to plan ahead and to execute your plan. It takes discipline to look objectivity at the end results, it takes discipline to change your plans accordingly if the results do not suffice.

It takes discipline to remain cool, calm, and collective when the world around you throws unsolicited opinions at your feet. It takes discipline to not react but instead respect the opinions of others. It takes discipline to put your pride to the side. It takes discipline to accept that you don't have all the answers to all the questions.

Discipline Requires Immediate Action

Discipline is a constant human awareness that feeds on action. Without action, there is no discipline. Doing it today, right now, takes discipline. Doing it tomorrow is procrastination. The nagging voice inside your head that says, I'll do it tomorrow, is the voice of procrastination. Procrastination is the bad habit of putting tasks off until the day after tomorrow what should have been done the day before yesterday. Procrastination says later, tomorrow, whenever I get a chance, when I feel like it, when this happens or when that happens. Procrastination also says, do what is necessary to get by, do what you can and nothing more.

In any given situation, we are constantly presented with these two choices. The choice to do it now or the choice to do it later. The voice in us that says do it tomorrow is the voice of procrastination. The voice in us that says do it now, is the voice of discipline.

The disciplined mind says do it now, do it right and do it to the best of your ability today, tomorrow and always. Discipline bears the seeds of achievement and success. Procrastination, on the other hand, bears the seeds of the easy life, for which the future will bear no fruits.

The rewards of a disciplined life are far greater, but they're often delayed. The rewards for the lack of discipline (procrastination) are immediate, but they are minor in comparison to the immeasurable rewards of a self discipline life. An immediate reward for lack of discipline is a fun day at the golf course. A reward of discipline is owning the golf course.

Pay The Price Of Being Disciplined

Success is nothing more than a few disciplines practiced daily. So, how can you master the art of self discipline? How can you get rid of distractions? How can you keep your mind on what you're trying to accomplish? How can you keep an attitude of doing it all and doing it now? How can you make the choice of discipline over procrastination? How can you avoid gossip? How can you stay focused on your goals and ambitions? How can you beat procrastination? How can you be decisive?

Simple, make the choice to get disciplined. Get discipline by working on being disciplined every day. Get discipline by making a conscious decision to be comfortable with being uncomfortable. Be disciplined by making it a habit of doing things now. Get disciplined by working on yourself on a daily basis. You have to make it a goal to be disciplined. It's not going to be an easy habit to cultivate, but nevertheless, it's achievable.

Anyone can be disciplined, but most people would rather sleep in until noon, rather than wake up at 5 in the morning. It's easier to go to bed late, show up late, leave early than it is to go to bed early, show up early and stay until the very end. It's easier to turn on the t.v. than it is to sit down and read a book. It's easier to do the bare minimum than to go above and beyond. It's easier to wait than it is to act.

Eventually, you'll have to pay the price. The price of discipline or the price of regret. One costs pennies the other a fortune. It's your choice to make.

It's Choice Time

We must all endure one of two things, the pain of discipline or the pain of regret. The pain of discipline bears seeds of achievement and success. The pain of regret, on the other hand, bears seeds of disappointment and failure. You have to make the choice of which of the two pains you are willing to endure.

With that being said, starting today, what are you willing to do to positively change your life? If you don't do something today that'll make an impact in your life, you can guess what the next couple years of your life are going to turn out like.

Here's a hint, look at the last couple years of your life, because the next few years are going to be exactly like the last couple of years of your life. Unless you, today, make the choice to change. You can choose to change it all, or change a little, or choose not to change at all. It's all up to you. Even so, it's nice to know that any day you wish, you can make the decision to change your entire life.

18

LIVE WITH A SENSE OF URGENCY

The truth is, many of us go through life with our emergency brakes on. We play it safe and cool by putting things off for "tomorrow" while ignoring and letting great opportunities slip by. Why do we do this? Because of a false sense of eternity. As conscious beings, we tend to avoid and dismiss the reality of life. We live and breeze through life as if we are immortal beings. But in reality, each one of us is living on borrowed time.

If you were to take the time out and think things through, you would quickly come to the realization that death is what fuels life. Knowing for sure that there's a finish line at the end of the race is a motivating feeling. It gives one purpose and a sense of urgency. Whether you decide to do something extraordinary or mediocre with your life, your number will eventually be called upon. It's inevitable. You might as well give it all you've got.

Act Now!

Stop living your life as if you have a thousand years to live. You're either here today or gone tomorrow. How many close friends and loved ones do you know that left this earth unexpectedly? If you're lucky, the answer is zero. But in fact, the answer is unbearable. It's a period of testing and agony. Where one is forced to come face to face with the harsh reality of life.

It's an empty and deflating feeling coated with self doubt and denial. A sad reality that takes place every passing day. It can undoubtedly shake up one's life for the worse. It can also instill the urge of urgency in one's life. Fearing it only adds fuel to the fire. Accepting it and coming to terms with it propels you forward.

Times Ticking. . .

There is no perfect time to do something. The time will never be just right. No matter what your circumstances might be at the time, one thing is for certain. Time doesn't stop nor wait for anyone. Riches or no riches, the sun will eventually set on us all. It's best to act now. Don't focus or worry about the how. Instead, focus all your energy and drive on your goals and vision. Everything else will soon fall into place.

It's up to you to take charge and control of your life. You can't sit around pouting and hoping things change. In order for things to get better, you have to be willing to make that choice to change. One simple idea can change your life forever. If you don't act first, life will. So stop wasting valuable time and energy on things that won't matter once you're gone. All your insecurities, imperfections, doubts and fears will soon be buried with you if you let them.

Accept them all and come to peace with them. In the unforeseeable future, everything and everyone you ever known, will eventually perish into the unknown. So cherish the today's of life

Take Action

A vision without any action is merely a dream. A vision with action can change the whole world. It's the action that counts. Everything can change today depending on what you choose to do. Don't wait until it's too late to do the things you want to do in life. Act with urgency in all areas of your life. Put the thoughts and opinions of others on mute. They too are on the same boat as you. Nobody has all the answers figured out. It may seem like it, but we're all winging it as we go. Some people just do a great job at it.

Their opinions and thoughts of you will eventually dictate your life if you let them. You're the one that has to live with the outcome of each decision you choose to make. Don't wait until the very end to ignore and silent your critics. Tune them out now. Especially the one inside your head. The one that constantly tries to belittle and hinder you from reaching and achieving your greatest potential.

Once you defeat yourself, you simultaneously defeat your greatest enemy. All your doubts, fears, anxiety and worries will gradually but surely disperse into the abyss. Confidence and self fulfillment will rise as a result.

Tips on how to live with a sense of urgency:

- Don't panic, stress or lose sight of your goals/vision
- Acknowledge and accept death
- Value and prioritize your time
- Know where and who to turn to for advice
- Make decisions with confidence and act on them promptly
- Identify obstacles and handle them a.s.a.p
- Establish a solution-based mindset
- Clarify the consequences of inaction
- Display urgency in your body language
- Learn how to say no
- Celebrate small achievements
- Think for yourself
- Meditate and exercise daily
- Get to the point and encourage others to do the same

We Are All Destined For Greatness

You have been created as one of a kind. You have been created in order to make a difference. Every single thing you do matters. You posses within you the powers needed to change the world. When you know exactly what you want to pursue in life, and want it bad enough, you will find a way to achieve it. The greatest adversity that you'll ever have to face in life is with your own ignorance.

With that being said, most people don't want to start due to the fear of being seen starting at the bottom. Whether that be at the gym, at work, a new business venture or at school, take the initiative and make that call. You'll thank yourself later. If you fail, congratulations, most people won't even try. Don't be like most people, make that choice and gain back control of your life. Let others lead small lives, but not you. Let others sob over small things, but not you. Let others quarrel over small things, but not you. Let others leave their future in someone else's hands, but not you. You're uniquely engineered and predestined to achieve greatness.

However, it's up to you to decide what's worth your while. Nobody else can make that choice for you. Time is of the essence, so stop wasting your valuable time and energy trying to imitate and replicate someone's else vision.

Instead, focus your time and energy on YOUR own visions and goals. Understanding and acknowledging this is key to living with a sense of urgency. All you have to do is release your emergency brakes and watch life unfold right in front of your eyes.

One day, anything and everything you ever envisioned in your life will soon manifest itself into the physical world. You just have to be willing to put in the time and effort. Lastly, in order to truly succeed, you must be willing to take the risks others won't. Being successful is all about testing out new ideas and taking risks.

Bear in mind, that when you take risks, you'll discover that there will be times where you succeed, and there will be times where you fail. Not all of your ideas are going to be million dollar ideas. Some ideas are going to result in great opportunities, while other ideas simply lead back to the drawing board.

Even so, don't let the fear of failure hinder you from taking risks in the future. As Emanuel Rohn once said, it's all risky. The minute you were born, it got risky. Going into business is risky, investing your money is risky, getting married is risky, having children is risky. It's all risky. I'll tell you how risky life is, you are not going to get out alive. That's risky!